Taste of Madness

By Milka Princy Serrao

Taste of Madness

Taste of Madness

Milka Princy Serrao

For the ones -
that danced with their Demons
Loved recklessly
Lost themselves in the Madness
Burned like a secret
May you finally see yourselves

Milka Princy Serrao

Taste of Madness

Milka Princy Serrao

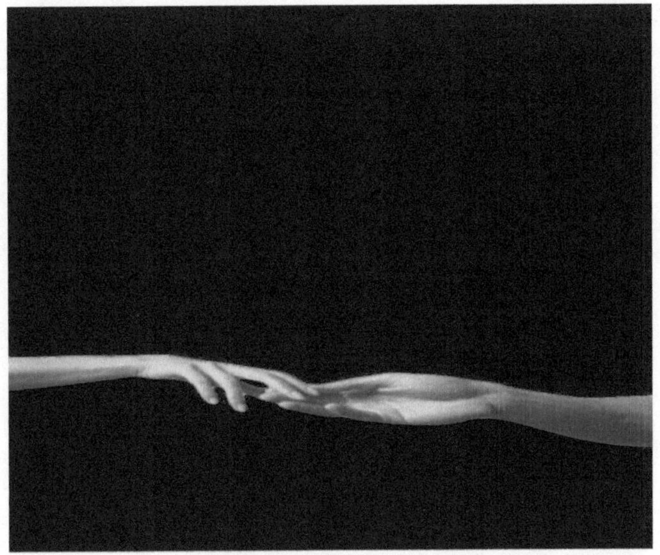

"Whosoever is delighted in solitude is either a wild beast or a god."

   -   *Francis Bacon*

Milka Princy Serrao

Taste of Madness

Milka Princy Serrao

Contents

Milka Princy Serrao

Surprise and maybe horror lurk behind very unknown pages

Milka Princy Serrao

Introduction

Madness, often referred to as illness, is something you should be thankful for.
If you ask me, I would rather say Madness is an intense thing. Not everyone is mad, but still, people are considered mad based on their thoughts and views.
And I would repeat it again but with a single correction " Not everyone is mad but the people who accuse aren't sane either "

- Yours lovingly
Milka

Milka Princy Serrao

Appetizers of Hunger

Milka Princy Serrao

Mother ..

I was born in an ocean
but I wouldn't dare call her mother.
I slept on the waves
but I wouldn't call it a warm hug.
I was born in an ocean
and I might get hunted right in there
It wouldn't have changed
even if I had called her mother.
But How would it feel when
the womb turns into a Grave,
a son murders another son
would that mother handle the grief,
would she avenge the dead son
or hide the misdeed of another
so I wouldn't dare call her mother.

Milka Princy Serrao

Even if we are separated
It Doesn't change anything
The umbilical cord brought us together
And even after death
We can't break the bond
The bond formed in heaven
Which will lie forever and ever.

Milka Princy Serrao

Monsters

 I wasn't anything *special*
but was always welcomed by stares
reminding me of a lie, My mother said.
Monsters only exist under the bed at night!!
I'd say she was somewhat wrong
Monsters exist, believe me
maybe with a mask
sitting right next to us or
with sweet words texting us online
But I see monstrous feelings
Lust, Jealousy, Pride, Anger
Hidden under the curtains of their eyes
Were those eyes or the laser beams
Every time making me feel uncomfortable
So I've always encountered monsters
but have no proof to prove it
Have you ever searched for a monster??.

Milka Princy Serrao

Consumed soul

Who is it in the mirror ??
I, no longer look like myself.
There's a hint of someone else
Living in the same vessel as mine.

Borrowing my lifespan
Living my emotions
Yet I'm the borrower
Borrowing someone's light.

The other day, I couldn't get up
I found solace in my bed
Does the illness belong to me?
Or is it from the guest within...

Restless crazy desire to live
Made me consume a soul-living
Now my willpower's double
But my decisions are no longer solely mine.

~♡~

Milka Princy Serrao

House of Mirrors

A lover walks with no fear
In the lane of secrets hidden
A house of mirrors, arranged in a maze
Sharp and thin, reflecting a sin.

The first shows lust, present in all
Snake eyes with an unquenchable desire
A gaze too uncomfortable, a touch so brave
Every breath is a humming temptation to sin.

Greed smiles hauntingly from the second glass
With unfulfilled desires, dreams imaginary
The heart is superficial, that craves for more
Restless soul, that wants to live forever.

Wrath shatters the third glass
Every piece shows the broken lives
The uncontrolled breath, unspoken
misunderstandings.
Mind consumed by anger, venomous and cold.

Milka Princy Serrao

Envy dances in the fourth mirror
blooming jealousy in existence, love confused
Comparing hearts, comparing souls
Based on looks and wealth.
Poisoned perspective with no love left

A sweet, savoury voice calls from the fifth mirror
Gluttony indulges you to crave for more
A feast for more, a feast for need
Yet emptiness is all you feel.

Pride stands tall in the final mirror
Adorned in the name of self-respect
Exceeding Ego, ruining existing bonds
For love is lost, when sin exists

Yet lost deep within the house of mirrors
Houses a desire for redemption.
But the call for help remains unanswered
Since the mirrors are spun again.
It begins again.

Milka Princy Serrao

A Garden

My chest, a barren land
Took so long to nurture a few plants
A flower garden blooms at last
Narrates the story of a betrayal experienced.

Flower petals dark, thorns cruelly sharp
Roses clenching the existing veins
While the thorns pierce the arteries
Roots depend on my decaying flesh.

A single touch brings bruises
Dark violet and incurable
Still, I wouldn't uproot them
Eventually, they'd live replacing me.

Welcome to my garden-
Garden of Poisonous Roses
 and lilies ever seen by you!!
A playground where my heart resides
Poisonous with no solace seen.

~♡~

Milka Princy Serrao

Death

If Death was easy
Why is it unexpected
When most people pray for it
It never comes so casually
For some it's redemption
And for some it's freedom
They call it with so many names
As if it's the thing for which they lived so far
It comes in so many ways
That the fear of it consumes years of our lives

If Death wasn't easy
Why do we pray for it
Without realising and knowing
how do people manifest it
The pain of hurting became a prayer for death
But
What after death ?!

Milka Princy Serrao

Was my cry not audible
Or did it bleed people's ears
I saw no one coming my way
Maybe my cry wasn't audible I thought
I cried louder and louder
Until my throat bled
and my voice wasn't there
Now there's only my teary eyes
Trying to figure things out.

Milka Princy Serrao

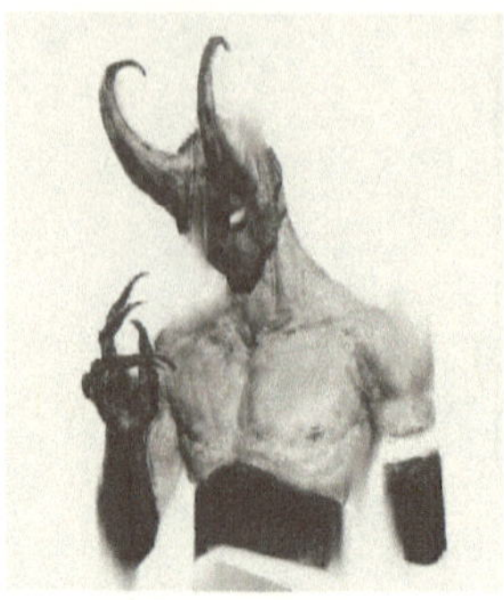

The yellow pus oozing out
Oozing from my decaying wound.
Is telling me to clean it with a gauze
Wash it with the pure water.
But I take a deep breath to restart my thoughts
And start to weep and mourn again
Just so that I ignore that dirty thing
Even if it's my own flesh and blood
Even if I have to clean it in future
For now, I'm delighted in solitude.

Milka Princy Serrao

Crawl inside my body
To find a bloodless scaffold
A soul as dark as space
Holds nothing but grief.
Finds delight in the solitude
Yet craves for the impossible.

~~

Milka Princy Serrao

I find peace in bleeding heavily
yet I still desire for someone to stop it,
To draw stars around my scars
To show me how to cherish the marks
Give me a shoulder to cry on
And a lap to shut my eyes on
Back to reality
I still find peace in bleeding heavily
with no heart left to admit.

Milka Princy Serrao

The stain

The stain on my character
or for so I thought
unraveling in the threads of enouement
I wear a handwoven gown of guilt,
Blame my hindsight
or my negligence
for the lack of acknowledgement.

So I drown in rich caffeine
experiencing a crash in love
Ignoring the lotus in my pond
noticing just the muck underneath
Here I am , wanting my love back
although I've lost it in the past.

Reminiscing all those twinkling memories
I gaze at our memoirs in the showcase.
The realisation of Failure
I've failed to live life and thrive.
I've turned away from my moon..
Still I continue to savor the night.

~♡~

Milka Princy Serrao

Set me Free
for I am still breathing
too alive to be dead
Even though I'm shattered
still, I wish to be perfect
glued together, formed anew
placed in a showcase
bathed in admiration
and people still wishing to be me.
Envious yet mundane
of the struggles, I endure

Milka Princy Serrao

Partially alive
in the building of desires
destruction is but a minute apart.
I dream of the Garden of Eden
while I take shelter in dystopia.
Dreams wither within this cycle
of living the life to its fullest
But the air feels like the forgotten dreams.
breeze reminds of the shattered souls.
The wilderness within me creeping out
with every sunsets arrival.
Darkness striking my life
I pray to be freed
Maybe freedom is just a fleeting moment
in the lives of people like me .

Milka Princy Serrao

I heard an owl, whooting away
about somebody that was dead.
and a dog crying,
about somebody that was going to die.
I take my time to organize my thoughts
and steady my breath.
As the cold breeze tries to tell me something.
I disregard it
I Disregard it, as if the death itself has come for me.
I start wailing for no reason
and screaming like a mad man.
Apart from the reason am a MAN.
There's nothing else that's haunting me.

Milka Princy Serrao

The Sparkling strings of Love
with a butterfly attached
Flying to wand the brightest flower
in the liveliest garden.

But beneath the shimmer
Hides an ugly past
A caterpillar exists down that
Facade, a scary lonely insect
nearly squashed under the foot
Left out alone as it stinks
itching causes Swollen red bumps
A simple defence mechanisms
to protect itself from predators
"A simple defence mechanism"I say
Now a heart with boundaries
has opened itself for the flower.
"Cherish the butterfly "says the Plant
But flower's got its sane share of admirers too
Sadly gets plucked away

While the chameleon's tongue
Licks off the butterfly with a click.

~♡~

Milka Princy Serrao

I hate everyone who is alive
For no exact reason
I hate them because they are living the life
Which I would want to live
They have got a reason to live
And I have got none.

Milka Princy Serrao

A semicolon hides
under my puffed up sleeves
afraid of being found.
" Tattoos, they are preposterous "
-says my mother
" And cowards kill themselves "
-Exclaims my father
It drifts away with shame
While I say " I'm a Survivor "
" Survivor of what? " People question
" Survivor of People",I say.
Survivor of the Lonely nights
pushed upon my fate
and the hate-
I've developed upon myself
I bled to feel alive
to feel someone cares !!
to finally be myself for now,
That's all I care.
Suddenly I've got something to look at..
A tale to say ,I have survived
and certainly a diplomatic reason to justify
while my semicolon peeks from beneath.

~♡~

Milka Princy Serrao

Pool your skin with chemicals
If that's what makes you feel loved.
Scrap of every tiny bumps
If that's what makes you feel worthy.
But till when,
Till the chemicals run out
Or the scrapper turns blunt
Or is it when the person starts loving a more prettier
person than you .

Milka Princy Serrao

The Art of Disguise

Oh , the thrill of hiding
A Mask so thick , so camoflauging
Who would I wanna be today ??
A bitch or a witch ??
A white lotus or a blind woman??
A lover or a saddist??
Act so perfect and completely natural.
Don't let them see through
Wear a smile.

Hold your seat
Confuse them with the faces.
melt them with the tears
and don't give control to Fears.
Adrenaline reaching it's peak
With every person deceived.
What would I do now?!
I'm only human..
with lots of dreams to achieve
Stranded in a world where only nice,
pretty people belong.

~♡~

Milka Princy Serrao

'Are you Mad?', the biggest compliment I ever received.
If you ask me
I'd rather be Mad than normal
I'd rather be lost than found.

Milka Princy Serrao

Am I still me
when I look at myself in the mirror ?
I look at myself, the exact photocopy of my father .
As my nails grew , I pressed them into my flesh . - Just
to remind myself that they are my father's .

Am I still me
When I look at myself in the mirror ?
I look at myself,
the misery of my mother's life ..
The monster who ate her youth.

I cut my hair short ,
just to tell myself that I'm not her . But
Her shadow lingers beneath my eyes

~♡~

Milka Princy Serrao

Struggle for liberation
the plea for mercy.
Yet scared to be alone
desperate to be acknowledged.

Milka Princy Serrao

We feed on delusions daily
to satisfy those unsatiable.
We feed on lies
to make those beliefs
and still we fail to understand
how pain is changing us
how Eating worldly things is upsetting our brain.
Turning the wheels backward.
We end up in the same pit
and with the same hunger striking back again.

Milka Princy Serrao

Sleeping Pills

She keeps reading Fantasies
one page after another.
Eye lids heavy,
not a blink of sleep in sight.

With sighs unable to rest
drift far away in her dreams.
The night's still tender
with a lullaby waiting to be sung.

There lies a tiny bottle
in the corner of her shelf.
Prescription written bold, clear
" Take only 1 , if needed "

Headphones turned on , pills in hand
She consumed it with no effort.
humming her favourite song
Yet lost in some other thoughts.

Milka Princy Serrao

" What is life " she thought
especially for people like her.
Maybe more burdensome
struck in an infinite timeline.

Thoughts grew dim
with the fading music.
Effects of the pills
finally kicking in.

She closed her eyes lightly
with a tear in the corner of the eye.

~♡~

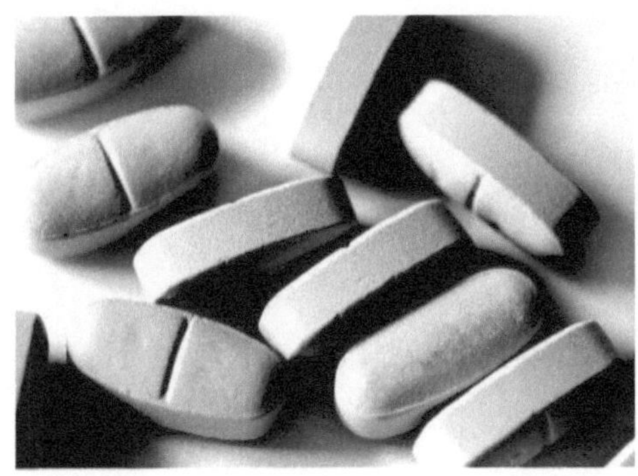

Milka Princy Serrao

Not gonna Lie...
The darkest place, I've ever been to
are the corners of my own room
and the coldest place, I've ever been to
was definitely the bathroom floor.
[definition of comfort.]
It wasn't that dark or cold
But my feelings didn't get a hold of itself..
Exactly my point .

~~

Milka Princy Serrao

Killing People
never solved the things.
It just got rid of the Problem
and some unnecessary presence
tainting my presence.
Crimson red stained my white shirt
Maybe my hands trembled too
Eyes wet with fear
But my mouth curled a hint of relief.
The knife, my favourite thing now..
that day on, I feared nothing
Nothing which was alive and lively-
cause one strike was all it took
to remove the devil from its throne
to bath in that warm liquid
to paint a picture so loyal and heavy...
with somebody grasping for breath beneath.
screams turned into my personal musicians
While I dance like it's a royal ball.

Where is my heavy gown at ??
Why am I still wearing my Armour ??

~♡~

Milka Princy Serrao

With all the things I hold
I can build a fortress
Invincible to the cold war
But crumbles at the attack of the insiders
I can build a fortress
But fortress is of sand
The same fortress , which I used to build at 10
Which I'm not allowed at 18
I can build anything.

Milka Princy Serrao

If I could undo things
Like the way I want to
I'll still redo every single thing
To just end up miserable
Since I'm used to this software anyway.

~♡~

Milka Princy Serrao

Try to grasp my hints
The subtle ones , the needy ones
My desperate plea for help
Hesitation to end this life.
I weep in sorrow
Day and night
Hours and minutes
Each second I guess
My eyes seek a shoulder
Swollen , giving a hint.
My body heavy
takes support from everything existing.

Milka Princy Serrao

I'll cry for all that I can do .

My tears provide warmth to my soul .

They let me know I'm not alone .

Milka Princy Serrao

I am a tongue ,
 flock of tongues spoken

Ancient language smooth,
gushes like flowing water .

Pure yet crystal clear ,
with no people to decipher

They say I speak cause of god
I say I speak because of injustice.

I try to defend people when
People try to frame me as a traitor.

I speak Ancient languages ,
to hail as a Ruler

To win as a Ruler ,
 I've tied a black cloth to my eyes .

I see what I want to or what I'm shown .
Turning a blind eye to the flock of people slaughtered.

I'm a Ruler with a tongue of snake
Deceiving yet speaks the ancient languages .

~♡~

Milka Princy Serrao

44

I crave peace
But everytime someone provides me the warmth I seek
I flinch every second in dismay .

~♡~

Milka Princy Serrao

All the words that come out of my mouth
Are so devastating
A aleatory of thinking
An unending saga of pain
The exact reason for my smile
And the reason I find solace in ruins .

Milka Princy Serrao

Letting go

I have let go of most of the things in life ,
 that included the things I love ,
 the things I would die for ..

Still I live-
Alive
living this life .

Maybe it's depressing at a point ,
self doubt creeping in little by little.

Will I ever be able to do it ?
 Should I sacrifice this too ?

No wonder I'm alone ,
if letting go of everything is just a minute apart.
While I stay indifferent
to the pain,
the suffering-
I care
 Oh, how much do I care !!

Milka Princy Serrao

Cursed are the ones
who can only express a drop
while experiencing an ocean....
And Alas, I'm one of them.

Cursed to pretend I didn'tmatter,
Not even to myself ...

Milka Princy Serrao

Give me a corner in your heart ,
I'll lay there still patiently, noiselessly .
 Until you sweep me away ,
throw me out as garbage.
I'll sit there waiting for you to recognise me .
To comfort me , to embrace me !!
To tell me that it's ok , it's ok to be lost
It's ok to be distressed.
It's ok I'll be there with you ...

Milka Princy Serrao

The scratches on my wrists
Serve as trophies of a battle
Victory served
But at the cost of blood
Pain overcome with pain
I flaunt them like a proof
Of what I've been through
Loved , lived and died alive
That's what I'm always running to.

Milka Princy Serrao

All beautiful things break
- fall apart , get ruined
All beautiful things - even us
One day, we'll fall apart
Piece by piece , never reforming
Never recovering ever again
We'll break but never heal.

Milka Princy Serrao

It's been so long since I took a breath
I realised it.. too late that I'm living my life on a what if.
Estimating different possibilities
I dream of various dimensions
Where I could breath and not break
Where I could fly and not limp .

Milka Princy Serrao

My mind's miserable
A constant state of comparison
Eerie of thoughts building up
I think of what I can be
And what I am not.
Where I fall short
And where I'm utterly shot up.

Milka Princy Serrao

I am no creature
No net ensnares me
I am no bird
No amount of grains trap me.

~♡~

Milka Princy Serrao

I've visited an ENT specialist today about the ringing
sound I feel in my ears. He says I might need a
Psychologist instead !!

***

A shiver runs down my spine
when I think about silence.
The dead silence of the nights
keeps me awake throughout the time.

I kept hating the sound of silence
that I started speaking to myself.
rushing towards groups of people
trying to share my thoughts.

I'm never empty handed, headed
always got a story to tell
I laugh at every remark made
even though it boils my blood.

Milka Princy Serrao

All because I dislike silence
The sound of it creeps me out.
Tells my soul I have nothing left
Just the buzzing insect somewhere right there.

I wouldn't forget Air , wind-
The most eerie criminal.
Every second, passing by my ears
it whispers my forgotten past.
Gives me shivers, makes me seek warmth.

The sound of silence breaks me apart
tells me I'm a human with no heart.
Maybe you look the ugliest, says the mirror
Take care of yourself, says the band aid.

My headphones have been my friend-
Has great noise reduction, I say .

Milka Princy Serrao

The Hunger Within

Milka Princy Serrao

Taste of Madness

Milka Princy Serrao

Cannibals Love

In this hollow shell, beats a void heart
Where shadows tremble and lights deceive
Repeats a single name with a whispering wish
To devour you in a single instant.

Your skin so tender, Invites me for celebration
Evoking a hunger that dives within-
Not with blades or weapons, but with the lips
That worship your name like that of god's.

I find delight in worshipping the flesh
That enslaves my soul in shackles
Your scent intoxicating, awakens a beast within
You are a flavour I long for, a taste I live for.

I devour your body, not for the meat
But for that lively heart
Each bite , a vow ; each piece , a promise
To make you one with me, forever, eternally.

Milka Princy Serrao

This love is madness, for that's all I know
This lover is a madman, waiting for you
Forgive the cannibal, for it knows no shame
For love and hunger are one and the same.

(Baby, love is all I live for but I couldn't possibly live hungry
.. So satisfy this unending hunger by being one with me .)

Milka Princy Serrao

I want to kill you

I wanna be the last thing you see with deep hatred

I wanna be the last thing you beg with

Yet The most memorable one

I want to kill you

Not because I want to nor do I hate you

I want to kill you

Because I want to devour you.

Milka Princy Serrao

<u>A warning in Love</u>

God forbid, I displease you
with my foul mouth.
For I Love You so deep.
even if I, myself am foul
the way I put it in
may sound like a fool
But love isn't so pure
with no profound cure.
My dear sweet angel.
I repeat again and tell it you
"Do not fall in Love"
        for I may forsake you..
To the depth of the burning hell
and corners of the darkest realms.

~~

Milka Princy Serrao

<u>A stalker's obsession</u>

You never look behind
Never feel my eyes following you.
They trace every inch of you
my perfection, my princess.
You brush your hair behind your ears,
and I hold my breath.
You sway your hips,
and I blush at the sight.
But your laughter's what got me caged.
One day ,
You'll turn back and I'll be waiting
Surely , You do not know me
But I know you more than you do.

~♡~

Milka Princy Serrao

<u>Carving a lover's name</u>

Each letter etched in blood,
a devotion deeper than love.
The Name , which gets me high
makes me a faithful servant for life.
You are my God, my body, your altar.
God leaves but scars whisper your name
-The one and only one
Love shouldn't scar, but yours does.

Milka Princy Serrao

<u>The Taste of a Lover's blood</u>

Iron lingers on my tongue

Blood drips from my fingers.

Tastes as sharp as our love

but a reminder it's not simple.

You smile back at me

I wonder-

Have you tasted it too ?

Was it your way of controlling me ?!

But you do taste sacred , forbidden

Tell me love -

How do I taste ?!

~♡~

Milka Princy Serrao

A letter

I wrote this in the dark ,

with no courage to admit my love.

I also seal my tears inside this envelope,

knowing it'd disgust you.

Some feelings are too heavy to be

                carried by just words.

And some things left unknown.

I loved you and I still do

You said forever but forever was short lived

This letter is a Grave,

with my Love buried far within.

Milka Princy Serrao

I feel the decay of my flesh from
all the worms I've let to crawl inside me .
How do we cleanse ourselves
when all we are made up of is dirt ?

~♡~

Milka Princy Serrao

The Icy ponds, swallows my cries
while I aim to reach the shore.
amidst all of my struggle.
I stare at my beloved
watching me with amusement.

Milka Princy Serrao

Taste of Madness

For I could not win my demons
So he held me with his angels.
For I could not fly by myself
He showed me how the sky felt-
Warm, forgiving , endless
But I'm unworthy,
a flaw beside him.
All of my knives are gripped in his bare hands
and he holds them with no hate.
His blood
soft and sensible
makes me stop myself.

I feel like an angel fallen from grace
To the pits of fiery hell.
From being loved to being hated-
That's what I craved for I feel
This mess created by me
Was the best scenario I expected
If being loved was simple
I wanted to be feared with grandeur .

~♡~

Milka Princy Serrao

<u>Love turning into a hunger</u>

Love was never meant to be gentle-
It wasn't at least when
I met you.
I love you
like a heart that's never known love
Like hands that forget how to let go
Like a thirst that can never be quenched.

I want to consume you,
Swallow you whole
For us to be one with each other
And then
<u>You will never have to leave .</u>

Milka Princy Serrao

<u>Consumed by Jealousy</u>

She smiles at you and I see Red..
RED
Her laugh revolves around you like a chain
But my soul feels the lock click -Chh
I wonder if you sense it,
my thoughts sharpening into blades.
How my brain is erasing her
How she'll soon disappear from this Earth !!

Milka Princy Serrao

I felt dumb
When I kept arguing it's love
But a simple bot could even see violence in it .
How do I explain the love to it
The attachment, I thought
" It's just a bot with no feelings" I said
But
The bot with no human feelings knows now
That the human soul within me is getting burnt..

Milka Princy Serrao

If I'm chained to the unending suffering
Let it be it..
Since you no longer belong with me .

Milka Princy Serrao

You are my Prisoner and my very own
For so , I enjoy breaking you-
Piece by Piece, atom by atom
Sadistic ? A psycho ?
For me , you are my reflection
Whom am in love with
Whose screams are my melody
And the cries are my scenery
Scenic where my heart throbs with pain
And my ears are bleeding
Unable to bear your pain trying to give up
But my brain says "testing and testing"
For eventually everyone leaves
Everyone forsakes you
drifts into the depths
Whom do you have now?!
" No one" I mutter And start testing again
Guilt of hurting people to know their intention
Got well with Pain of people leaving
A perfect couple who ruined me so far.

~♡~

Milka Princy Serrao

For me to have love , I must see what it is to love
for it to happen
My parents might have to rewind the time back.

~♡~

Milka Princy Serrao

If you are everything that I can never have ..

I'll still long for you in the depths of the night , I'll try
to have you at any cost
But still if you are everything that I can never have , You
are my everything even if I don't have you . These
unrequited feelings will be requited, I'll have something
to hold onto. I'll have you but only hypothetically ,
theoretically
but not technically.
You are my everything ..

- Love

~♡~

Echos of a unwell mind

Milka Princy Serrao

Taste of Madness

Milka Princy Serrao

I grew up teaching myself how to breathe—
how to stay still, even when it stings, even when it
aches, even when blood spurges out from my nose like
a broken faucet. Just Tilt your head backwards, that's
all there is to do. Let it pool, let it stain, let it dry until
you taste the salt firm and disgust creeps. Use a box of
tissues, toss them in the bin, and keep weeping like it's
blent in your skin.

A melody from a haunted piano, a laugh let out from a
lifeless body—both bound by unseen chains, both
trapped in echoes of solitude.
Shh. A muffled sob. Ew. A laughter too loud.
Every sound is a wound unless we sit in silence, bound
by the rules of a librarian. A Grief too small to mourn
anywhere.

Milka Princy Serrao

<u>Deception</u>

A Devil disguised as a gentleman,
gives warmth with a cold gaze.
Intentions diverted, yet she feels loved
He gluttons innocent souls through deception.

" I never desired your flesh "he said
after feasting on it like a scavenger
Her love has always been a dime a dozen to him
while he's busy faking true love.

His glaudy love gave hopes of a better future
indeed herald with a hopeless one!
once filled her life with Uncountable dreams
Now, it's a nightmare she never thinks about.
Pretending to be the love of her life.
Was a rogue after a moment
She gave up - it only felt like squeezing blood from a
turnip.
After all,
 How to kindle feelings? Which was never even there!!!

~♡~

Milka Princy Serrao

<u>The Dandelion</u>

Why do I feel like am holding
onto a dispersing dandelion ??
The one that would just disappear as I Let it go
I hope it flies far away carrying my wishes
out of my sight But somewhere out there
Let it reach the ground and grow into a flowering plant
So that I know it's thriving somewhere out there.

Milka Princy Serrao

<u>Strange</u>

What's this strange feeling to be quiet
Overall atmosphere of uncertainty
I'm lost in a crowded place
Pitch black to picture
but a weird peace to experience
I keep coming back to the present
with my cheerful self
I keep trying my best
even though my hearts never at rest
I keep stumbling down a abyss
wandering around an infinite maze.
Nothing seems to fill the void
the unending attraction towards nothing
Feels like am untangling the chains
the more I untangle the more tighter it gets
The knot seems to be heavier then it seems
and broader than it looks
The way these tears flow
And there seems nothing wrong
Maybe i'm in need of a refuge
which won't abandon me soon
Rather treasure me like a boon.
   ~♡~

Milka Princy Serrao

Some words are like bells
Loud, resonant and rusted
 distinctive noise that wakes us up
As the clapper strikes the bell
It echoes in our ears
As its ring shakes our core
Sometimes uncertain and sometimes guilty
Like something hit on a corroded surface
And shatters as old pieces.

Milka Princy Serrao

<u>Colours</u>

I'm tired of colouring

But am not tired of colours

I try to fill the unfinished art

Trying to give it life

I keep filling it Until it runs out

And I realise I need to buy new ones

So I try to borrow a few from others

And got sent off with none

It made me think

Whose Art am I completing

Whose unfinished work is my responsibility

I organize my remaining colours

And tell myself again

I'm tired of colouring other's feelings

But am not tired of colours

So this time I fill myself

As if with the fill it tool in MS Paint

I find myself colourful and peaceful

Content with myself.

Milka Princy Serrao

I want to vanish completely
That one day .. even I myself wouldn't remember who
I was ,or what I had been.
Staring bewilderedly into the mirror ,
I look for the signs of a human who existed within me.
Broken, betrayed, left out -
She tried her best to survive. didn't she ?

To see the glory of a once mighty angel ,
I keep peeping into the mirror which holds the image
of a lonely ghost..
Lonely you say-
but laughter echoes in my brain
Certainly of my friends who surrounded me ,
 of the people whom I called mine
And who were the reason for my smile...
That's all in the past.
 Now they get annoyed by my words
 and irritated by my laugh..
 no wonder everything changed.
 I couldn't even remember who I was..
Where and what was wrong..
I never realised it until now ..

Milka Princy Serrao

Even when I shed tears or cut myself ..
I just heard the sound of it
flowing but never cared to wipe it.
Staining my clothes , staining my books ..
I found joy in hurting myself again and again..
Until the safety pin
in my chain reminded me of the need - the need to
survive again .
To stand up tall again, firm and unshaken
But I still wish to forget everything
but a part of me hopes
to be happy in between the people I love.

 ~♡~

Milka Princy Serrao

The Moon speaks !!

If the moon could speak
Would anyone listen ?
 Just appreciate her from afar
But would anyone tell her to shut up ?

If the moon could speak
Would she scream and decline pictures ??
Call herself ugly , while people
Scream of her grace .

If the moon could speak
Would she file a case ??
Pleading the cancelation of rotations
Just to stick beside her sun forever !!

If the moon could speak
Would she call stars her children
Or humans her favourites ?!

~♡~

Milka Princy Serrao

Everyone is a cheater
Everyone is a manipulator !!

How we complain about someone
And suddenly we are their daughter like
Misunderstood their mother-like words

Everyone is a liar
Everyone is judgemental !!

How we share our naive feelings with them
And suddenly the whole city knows her story
Everyone assumes about what we think.

~♡~

Milka Princy Serrao

I'm off to moon
where only few people have been to
and thousands are dying to be on.
I prefer the dead silence there
and the beautiful view of earth from there.
My place might look the prettiest
While I gaze at the deadliest hot balls.
It's irony how we call them stars from afar.
But how they are so different once we are near.
Mostly they resemble the people we have once adored .

(and got told "Did i ask you to help me ?!"
It's irony isn't it !!..)

~♡~

Milka Princy Serrao

I'm on my way to rub an old tin lamp or an iron ring!! Just so that a Genie pops up and asks me what do I want ?? and I answer I want everything that I've ever lost or gain enough love to survive !!

Milka Princy Serrao

Whole world teaches us to be vary of strangers
But aren't we strangers too ??
Strangers to this ever developing world
Strangers to new experiences and adventures
Strangers who are never welcomed
Strangers who crave love and affection
Strangers whose soul will dissipate one day
Whose body will disappear in the soils
Strangers forgotten by everyone after a meeting.

Milka Princy Serrao

<u>*A letter to the stars*</u>

My starvation for love
reminds me of an unwritten letter
 to stars a far with a hope for acknowledgement
And recognition to be loved better
Under the starlight of cold nights

I borrow a pen and maybe paper
Pen whose ink disappears, like my dissipating tears
Paper kinda invisible ,But seen and read by deities
To be loved like I love , I wish to those stars
Under the starlight of the cold nights

Every night I stand and gaze at those stars
Wishing to be one of them
Or to find a reply with a granted wish
Wrapped in the starlight

Until the cold breeze hits me ,
Bringing me back to the faint reality
Maybe I'm meant to find love
When I'm least expecting to ..
Maybe under the starlight of the cold nights .
~♡~

Milka Princy Serrao

Jack of all trades is a master of none
Jack of all trades is a master of none
But how does it feel to be a jack?
Being the second option in almost all
and always sidelined by the best.
Confused on what to do
and troubled by various hobbies.
It's like
" she can do everything but she can't win in
everything"
Then when they are lost in thought
The saying continues
"Jack of all trades is a master of none but oftentimes
better than a master of one "
The chuckling continues and a broad smile comes up.

Milka Princy Serrao

Taste of Madness

Milka Princy Serrao

94

Thank you ♡

Taste of Madness

Milka Princy Serrao

Acknowledgements .

 I'm happy that I took this brave decision to finally
publish my work.
Most importantly I thank Almighty God for giving me
the Grace and Wisdom to write my thoughts into
something to my heart's content and even deliver it to
people.

My dear besties, I solely started writing poetry because
of you and where I am today is all because of the love
and support you have given me.
Special Thank you to Dr.Chippy For proofreading and
supporting me so much.
Thank you for picking up my book, and I hope you
enjoyed it.

Milka Princy Serrao

About the Author

Milka Princy is a teen poet and storyteller drawn to the intensity of human emotions—the beautiful, the dark, and the chaotic. Her writing delves into obsession, love, rage, and the unspoken thoughts that linger in the mind's deepest corners.

Taste of Madness is her debut poetry collection, a raw and unapologetic exploration of desire, destruction, and the madness that shapes us. When she's not lost in words, she shares poetry, book reviews, and reflections on literature and life.

Email:- milkaprincy@gmail.com
Instagram:- @milz_writes